Book Synopsis

"KINGDOM SHIFTERS DECREE THAT THANG" is an apostolic decree booklet FOR ANYONE who desires to go higher in the rule and authority of prayer and contending for the promises of the Lord. The book focuses on deliverance and healing of the mind, body, spirit, and soul, shifting atmospheres, and establishing the kingdom of God in the earth realm. Learn the biblical purpose and power of decreeing and declaring, and how to effectively pray and utilize the scriptures in intercessory prayer. Learn how to establish, manifest and activate the scriptures and prophetic promises of the Lord in your life, lineage, ministry, and sphere of influence. Declare out written declarations that have been birth in the presence of the Lord and thus produce His will, character, and fruit in every facet of your life.

Kingdom Shifters Decree That Thang!

TaquettaBaker@Kingdomshifters.com

(Website) Kingdomshifters.com

Connect with Taquetta via Facebook or Youtube

Taquetta's Bio

Taquetta Baker is the founder of Kingdom Shifters Ministries (KSM). She has authored fourteen books and two decree CD's. Taquetta has a Master's Degree in Community Counseling with an emphasis on Marriage, Children and Family Counseling, a Bachelor's Degree in Psychology and Associates Degree in Business Administration. In addition, Taquetta has a Therapon Belief Therapist Certification from Therapon Institute and has 22 years of professional and Christian Counseling experience.

Taquetta is also gifted at empowering and assisting people with launching ministries, businesses and books and provides mentoring, counseling and vision casting through Kingdom Shifters Kingdom Wellness Program. Taquetta serves on the Board of Directors for New Day Community Ministries, Inc. of Muncie, IN.

In October 2008, Taquetta graduated from the Eagles Dance Institute under Dr. Pamela Hardy and received her license in the area of liturgical dance. Before launching into her own ministry, Taquetta served at her previous church for 12 years. She was a prophet, pioneer and leader of Shekinah Expressions Dance Ministry, teacher, member of the presbytery board, and overseer of the Altar Workers Ministry. Taquetta receives mentoring and ministry covering from Bishop Jackie Green,

Founder of JGM-Enternational PrayerLife Institute (Redlands, AZ), and was ordained as an Apostle on June 7, 2014.

Taquetta flows through the wells of warfare and worship and mantles an apostolic mandate of judging and establishing God's kingdom in people, ministries, communities, and regions. Taquetta travels in foreign missions and throughout the United States. She has mentored and established dance, altar workers, deliverance, and prophetic ministries. Taquetta ministers in the areas of fine arts, all manners of prayer, fivefold ministry, deliverance, healing, miracles, atmospheric worship, and empowers and train people in their destiny and life's vision.

Connect with Taquetta and KSM at <u>kingdomshifters.com</u> or via Facebook. For more information regarding Bishop Jackie Green at Jgmenternational.org.

Forward

In each generation, there are individuals who seem to come from nowhere and make an indelible mark on society. In many cases, once you examine the life of the person, it is clear that they were always headed toward greatness. Equally so, for many of those individuals, we can find that their perception of themselves had nothing to do with greatness and everything to do with a simple belief to be the right person doing the right thing at the right time such that others would be blessed. Taquetta is just that person for the present age in Christian ministry. She has definitely been strategically chosen by God to specifically challenge the stagnation of religious thinking and release a revival strategy of five-fold ministry. God is using those with a pure heart and clean hands to introduce His movement for the end-times church. The world is too polluted with its own wickedness, including a multitude who have been directly damaged by the traditions of the church such that it necessitates pioneers who believe in miracles, signs, and wonders, as well as a standard of excellence and a commitment to deliverance, healing, and completeness. Again, Taquetta is one of those pioneers that God has set in this church age. She is a believer in the vision that God is altogether who He declares Himself to be in His Word.

Through several years of dedicated fasting and praying and searching the Word, along with studying instrumental ministries such as Charles Spurgeon and Kathryn Kuhlman, Taquetta has come into her own of standing boldly in the kingdom. By having a copy of this book, you are being privileged to see the premiering of Taquetta's life almost as if you were sitting on Broadway with the best seat in the house and watching the curtain open to what is destined as a cultural icon of stage plays. As the author of her faith, God has put together chapter after chapter of what is absolutely purposed to become a Christian *bestseller. You will be challenged and changed. You will be blessed and elevated. You will be humbled and inspired. Whatever the totality of your response, one thing is guaranteed – you will be a better person for having read what God has inspired, first in a life and now in a book. Above all, I pray that you take away from this reading experience the impartation of taking what God has used to better you and giving out that others would be blessed. In that, you can say, "my life was shifted, transformed and elevated through the fullness of God's will being established in my life as I became a student of His promises, ordinations, and proclamations through this book." Now as Taquetta would say, "Go forth and decree that thang."*

Apostle Kathy E. Williams, Founder of New Day Community Ministries, Inc.

Taquetta's Content Page

DECREE THAT THANG!

God has anointed us with the divine authority to be able to literally transform any atmosphere with our very presence.

Isaiah 61:1-3
The Spirit of the Lord GOD is upon me; because the LORD hath anointed me to preach good tidings unto the meek; he hath sent me to bind up the brokenhearted, to proclaim liberty to the captives, and the opening of the prison to them that are bound; To proclaim the acceptable year of the LORD, and the day of vengeance of our God; to comfort all that mourn; To appoint unto them that mourn in Zion, to give unto them beauty for ashes, the oil of joy for mourning, the garment of praise for the spirit of heaviness; that they might be called trees of righteousness, the planting of the LORD, that he might be glorified.

When our presence generates a voice, God's power reigns with a vengeance that restores jubilee, dissolves prison gates, liberates the bound, reorders God's purpose and will, rekindles His holiness, and transports people into right order with God's plan and destiny for their lives and situations.

When God made the heaven and the earth, it was His very presence and voice that brought this world into existence.

Genesis 1:1-5
In the beginning God created the heaven and the earth. And the earth was without form, and void; and darkness was upon the face of the deep. And the Spirit of God moved upon the face of the waters. And God said, Let there be light: and

1

there was light. And God saw the light, that it was good: and God divided the light from the darkness. And God called the light Day, and the darkness he called Night. And the evening and the morning were the first day.

God's Spirit moved upon the form and void of the earth and upon the darkness of the waters, and once God's presence was in position, He spoke light into existence. God saw that the light was good and gave it a name that distinguished it from what already existed which was darkness. God further distinguished light by calling it day, but He even gave darkness its own name, night. He established both their purposes by saying, *"And the evening and the morning were the first day."*

When God speaks, He transforms and distinguishes. When God decrees, He establishes. He establishes not just what will be, but what was, and then gives both a purpose distinct one from the other. Once God establishes a purpose, it is a done deal, it is set in stone. It is finished. God cannot lie and refuses to go back on His word. When He decrees a thing, the very life of His words breathes its existence. As God's created image and chosen vessels, He has given us the same effective power. God has also given us the power to not only decree with our mouths, but to decree with our bodies (*His presence moved upon the face of the earth*). He has given us the divine ability to breathe life and declare life via movement and watch it form before our very eyes ***"And the evening and the morning were the first day."***

According to Webster's Online Dictionary, *Decree* is defined as:
1. an order usually having the force of law

2. a religious ordinance enacted by council or titular head
3. a foreordaining will
4. a judicial decision of the Roman emperor
5. a judicial decision especially in an equity or probate court

According to Webster's Online Dictionary, the definition of *Declare* means:
1. the act of declaring, announcement
2. the first pleading in a common-law action
3. a statement made by a party to a legal transaction usually not under oath, something that is declared
4. the document containing such a declaration

According to Webster's Online Dictionary, the definition of *Establish* means:
1. to institute (as a law) permanently by enactment or agreement, settle
to make firm or stable, to introduce and cause to grow and multiply
2. to bring into existence, found, bring abound, effect
3. to put on a firm basis, set up, to put into a favorable position, to gain full recognition or acceptance of
4. to make (a church) a national or state institution to put beyond doubt, prove

I would define decree as a biblical command that is in line with God's word and desires and conveys His will and purpose for a person or situation.

Job 22:28
You will also decree a thing, and it will be established for you; so light will shine on your way.

Declare in this passage of scripture is *Gazar*, which means:

1. to cut, divide, cut down, cut off, cut in two, snatch, decree
2. to cut off, destroy, exterminate
3. to decree
4. to be cut off, separated, excluded
5. to be destroyed, cut off
6. to be decreed

When we decree, we divide God's word from the enemy's and man's word by snatching down, cutting off, and destroying the power, strongholds, and limitations that prevent God's original state for creating us in His image from manifesting. We exterminate a present judgment, while establishing God's true judgment and law, His ultimate desires for our lives before the fall of man.

Established in this scripture is *Quwm* and means:

1. to rise, arise, stand, rise up, stand up
2. to arise (hostile sense)
3. to arise, become powerful
4. to arise, come on the scene
5. to stand
6. to maintain oneself
7. to be established, be confirmed
8. to stand, endure
9. to be fixed
10. to be valid
11. to be proven, ratify, impose
12. to be fulfilled, fulfill
13. to persist
14. to be set, be fixed
15. to raise, set up, erect, build
16. to raise up, bring on the scene
17. to raise up, rouse, stir up, investigate
18. to raise up, constitute
19. to cause to stand, set, station, establish
20. to make binding

21. to carry out, give
effect to

In this chapter, we have Eliphaz providing counsel to Job. Job was stripped of everything he had including family, possessions, and health, at the permission of God. Eliphaz's presumption was that Job had sinned and therefore, had caused God to judge him. Though Job had not sinned, Eliphaz was definitely correct in letting Job know that he had the power to speak life into his present situation, and God would restore and establish him greater than he was before the enemy was allowed to terrorize him. No matter how much Job complained, his decree was God is always greater than what was occurring in his life. Job took a stand and eventually saw the fullness of that decree manifest on his on his behalf. We can see from this scripture and the definitions, that decreeing has the power to push us into a greater strength and power that positions, carries out, and gives effect to God's defined plan and purpose for our lives.

Throughout the Bible those who made decrees were either authority figures, kings, or those who had great influence in their land (examples; Moses, David, Daniel, John, Peter, Jesus). Whether good or bad, when a decree is made, it is a done deal. It cannot be changed, not even by the person who declares it. We notice this in the story of Daniel and his Hebrew companions (See Daniel 3 & 6), who came into great adversity because of a negative decree concerning worshipping false gods. We also find in these stories that God showed Himself strong, and that new divine decrees were established to override the ungodly ones.

Elijah is another great example of God using a man of authority, a prophet, to make a prophetic decree. In 1Kings 17:1, God used Elijah to make a prophetic decree to Ahab stating,

"As the Lord God of Israel lives, whom, I serve, there will be neither dew nor rain in the next few years except at my word."

And indeed there was no rain in the land for the next few years. Following this drought, Elijah made this declaration to Ahab,

"Get up, eat and drink, for there is a sound of the abundance of rain" (1Kings 18:41).

Elijah did not just make the decree of rain randomly. He carried out the specific orders of God first. Then he made the decree of the abundance of rain. ***Sometimes, specific instructions will need to be carried out before some decrees can come to pass.***

As soon as Elijah made the declaration of *the abundance of rain (1Kings 18:41)*, it further fulfilled his previous declaration that *it would not rain again until he spoke it (1Kings 17:1)*. His very words set the heavenlies in motion for rain and transformed his nation.

When Elijah stated that he *heard the sound of the abundance of rain*, it was a spiritual hearing. The rain had not yet manifested nor was there even a cloud in the sky. Elijah's proclamation about hearing the rain was made according to what God had spoken *(go show yourself to Ahab and I will bring rain upon the earth).* and according to what Elijah could "hear" through the spirit of God. He heard the rain before it was and spoke it and it became so, much like God declaring day and night from what was and then it became. Within the Spirit, Elijah could hear the rain forming; so much so he went on the top of Carmel. This was a way of positioning himself to receive the full manifestation of the decree. Then he put his face between his legs and waited for it and had his servant look seven times for it. What was spiritual was becoming natural and Elijah could hear it forming with unwavering expectation.

1Kings 18:42-45
So Ahab went up to eat and to drink. And Elijah went up to the top of Carmel; and he cast himself down upon the earth, and put his face between his knees, And said to his servant, Go up now, look toward the sea. And he went up, and looked, and said, There is nothing. And he said, Go again seven times. And it came to pass at the seventh time, that he said, Behold, there ariseth a little cloud out of the sea, like a man's hand. And he said, Go up, say unto Ahab, Prepare thy chariot, and get thee down, that the rain stop thee not. And it came to pass in the meanwhile, that the heaven was black with clouds and wind, and there was a great rain. And Ahab rode, and went to Jezreel.

Jesus is another awesome example of one who knew His power and authority to decree and watched the breath of His words come to pass. All throughout His life on earth, Jesus would decree healing and miracles and they would form right before the people. Everything Jesus said was so and came to pass. Jesus was the Word which made His presence of authority all the more powerful.

This is the reason it is important for us to have the Word of God inside of us, so that what is in us can form from what is spoken through us. The following scriptures will give you a glimpse of a few of the decrees Jesus made:

> Mark 1:23-27 (Cast out unclean spirit)
> Mark 4:39 (Peace be still)
> Matthew 8:6 (Healed and cast out devils with his word)
> Matthew 20:16 (First shall be last and the last shall be first)
> Mark 14:28, 14:62, 16:17-118 (declares his resurrection)
> Mark 16:17-18 (Jesus declares that signs will follow believers)
> John 10:30 (I and my Father are one)
> John 11:25-26 (Jesus declares he is the resurrection and the life, etc.)
> oh 11:43 (Lazarus come forth)
> John19:30 (It is finished)
> Matthew 8 (Sending His word and healings occur)

DECREE VS. PROPHECY

Decreeing is built on Isaiah 55:11, which states, *"So shall my word be that goeth forth out of my mouth: it shall not return unto me void, but it shall accomplish that which I please, and it shall prosper [in the thing] whereto I sent it."*

Though some prophetic words are decrees, not every prophetic word is a decree. Prophecy is the promise, potential, and desired will of God (See 1Corinthians 14:3). Decreeing is the establishment of God's will, the institution of His promises, and when declared through prophecy it distinguishes "what is" from "what was," while providing an immediate manifestation of what will be.

Though prophecy can convey the will of God and *is a set in stone* word or directive, you have a choice of accepting or rejecting the word. Your choice can dictate whether God's will manifest in your life, or for a particular situation. But when God makes a decree, there is no choice. "IT IS SO!"

Decreeing reorders us to our original state of authority, position, and dominion (emotionally, spiritually, and physically) before Adam fell. It empowers heaven on earth by releasing and merging our heavenly kingdom with our natural lives.

PURPOSE OF DECREEING

- Covers and establishes the mantle of the word
- Immerses us in the principles of God's word
- Refreshes and revitalizes prophecies that have been spoken over our lives.
- Releases and dislodges those words and goods that have been stored or held up in the Spirit realm (Daniel 10)
- Births forth decisions and yields conclusions to the matter at hand.
- Establishes spiritual laws that bring about a natural good or necessary purpose.
- Brings security in what God has said to, for or through us.

HOW TO DECREE

- Decrees must be spoken from a place of authority. One must be confident in whom he or she is in God and rooted in faith that God never goes back on His word.
  - *(Matthew 11:12 And from the days of John the Baptist until now the kingdom of heaven suffereth violence, and the violent take it by force).*
- We can decree through our bodies via movement, so be open to God leading you to perform a prophetic act while decreeing, or to dance or dramatize a decree. I minister this way a lot during praise and worship and in my personal time of prayer and intercession. At times, movement and prophetic acts, aide in bringing release and fullness to what God is birthing and establishing.

- What we decree MUST be the will, heart, and mind of Christ...not our desires, presumptions, or opinions.
- We cannot continue to just speak things into the atmosphere and hope they come to pass. Decrees must be spoken within the Spirit realm. The person must enter the Spirit and command those things in the Spirit to be made flesh in their natural lives. The Spirit realm is as close as you believe it to be. If you believe it to be a matter of batting an eye, you will enter at that level of faith. If you believe the Spirit realm is far away, and you have to pray it into existence, then you will enter at that level of faith. Since we are spiritual beings and are to be living spiritual lives, I would encourage you to acquire a revelation of the spirit realm being right at your disposal…right at the blink of an eye…or that you are so enmeshed that even a blink is not necessary, as this allows you to be one with God, and increases your level of access to Him, His presence and His every kingdom good you desire or need.
- I would encourage you to pray until God releases your Spirit. Often, we will make loose statements into the heavenlies or we will pray and make decrees concerning matters, but we end the prayer without God yielding a release in the Spirit. Though decrees are established, at times, we must battle in prayer to see them come to pass. The Holy Spirit provides a release so that we will know that what we have prayed/decreed has been taken care of and to elevate us to another level of faith. *Sometimes we abort manifestation because we fail to pray without ceasing or we fail to pray through to a*

place of completion with God. After making your decrees, praise and worship or even wait quietly until God releases you from the prayer.

When we decree we are scribing (establishing). We are giving an account of God's goodness and ability and we are eternally publishing His works and will, His promises and proclamations for our lives and those we minister to. God put power in our mouths, hands and feet so that we could set the captives free and be establishers of His kingdom. As movers and shakers of the kingdom, we must be open to how God desires to use us and be available to decreeing His will, so the fullness of our destinies and His kingdom can manifest in the earth.

NOW GO FORTH & DECREE THAT THANG!

MY DAILY PORTION

Lord, open my spiritual and natural senses and vision in a greater dimension as I move in my gifts and calling.

I decree I have Your eyes and see Your visions; I have Your ears and hear Your desires and strategies for each gift that I have.

I decree Jesus that I sense Your presence and submit my gifts to be used how You desire me to use them, Lord.

I submit my mind and thought processing and think confidently that I can do and convey everything You show me and tell me Lord.

With my entire being, I surrender my heart and spirit to You Lord, and command them to increase with a yearning to want to minister and magnify you in the greatest depth possible.

I renounce the spirit of discouragement and frustration and believe Your word that says I can do all things through You Lord; You are my strength.

As I surrender my gifts to Your strength and Holy Spirit, Lord. Let every gift flow easily and interchangeable within my ministry.

Lord significantly and efficiently increase my creativity and yield in abundance the ability for me to make your word and will flesh within my ministry.

Lord let me learn with ease, receive correction with ease, and seek excellence as I utilize my gifts for Your kingdom and glory.

Raise the power level in my gifts and ministry Lord. Let Your transformation power reign and leak in an outpouring from my gifts and from my ministry.

Let each of my gifts embrace and transform for Your good all who encounter it.

Get Your glory Lord out of my gifts and ministry as a whole.

EXOUSIA WORD POWER

In the beginning [before all time] was the Word (Christ), and the Word was with God, and the Word was God Himself! I decree the word is me, is with me, and ministers through me. I am the word of God himself (Jn 1:1).

I decree that Your word Lord is a lamp to my feet and a light to my path. As I minister, Your word shines forth and exposes darkness while bringing healing light and direction to Your people. (Psa 119:105)

My heart is inditing a good matter: I speak and minister the things which I have made touching the king (Psa 45:1).

Every Scripture is God-breathed, given by His inspiration, and profitable for my instruction, reproof and conviction of sin, for correction of my errors and discipline in obedience, and is my training in righteousness in holy living, in conformity to God's will in thought, purpose, and action for my life (2Tim 3: 16).

I decree that I will write the visions that the Lord downloads to me and will make them plain so that those partaking of my ministry will receive a clear vision of what the Lord is speaking (Hab 2:2).

I decree that I will delight myself in Your statutes Lord: I will not forget Your word and will study Your word when preparing myself to minister (Psa 119:16).

I decree that my eyes are open, beholding the

wondrous things out of Your law Lord (Psa 119: 18).

I decree that out of my belly and the heart of my gifts, shall flow rivers of living water (Jn 7:38)

I decree that the word I have laid up in my heart is cleansing and establishing Your voice and presence in me, that I might not sin against You Father God (Psa 119:11).

I decree that even as every word of God is tried and purified, He is shielding me as I trust and take refuge in Him (Pro 30:5).

For God's spoken Word is alive in me and full of Dunamis power. I decree God's word is active, operative, energizing, and effective in every aspect of my life and ministry.

I decree that God's word in me is sharper than any two-edged sword, penetrating to the dividing line of the breath of my life (soul) and spirit, and of my joints and marrow, exposing, sifting, analyzing, and judging the very thoughts and purposes of my heart and those I minister to and with (Heb 4:12).

Therefore, I will meditate on Your precepts Lord and have respect to Your ways for I know the paths of life have been marked out for me by Your law (Psa 119:15).

For the sky and earth will pass away, but my God's words will not pass away (Matt 24: 35); His word is eternal and is producing His ordained will for my life.

I therefore study Your word so that I can be delivered of all uncleanness and the rampant outgrowth of wickedness, so that in a humble, gentle, modest spirit, myself and others can receive and welcome the Word which has been implanted and rooted in our hearts with power to save and transform souls (Jam 1: 21).

I decree wholehearted that I will be a mature doer of God's Word and obey His message. I decree I will not merely just listen to it, betraying myself and others, but will feast on it such that deception is cast down and truth is exalted in my life and ministry (Jam 1: 22).

I decree I will delight to do Your will, God; yes, Your law is within my heart and leaks from my ministry (Psa 40: 8). I delight in You and am invested in what concerns You and bring You joy and fulfillment.

For I decree Your word that is in me Lord, shall go forth out of my mouth and the lions of my ministry, and it shall not return to You void. I declare Your word through me shall accomplish that which You please and purpose, and it shall prosper in the thing for which You my matchless King hath sent it (Isa 55: 11).

You have seen what I need and desire Lord, and You are hastening Your word to perform it in my life (Jer 1:12).

THE BLOOD OF JESUS

The blood of Jesus is essential in purifying yourself before the Lord. It is essential to repent & cleanse in the blood of Jesus daily to purge sin from your ministry.

> ### Hebrew 9:22
> *Amplified*
> *[In fact] under the Law almost everything is purified by means of blood, and without the shedding of blood there is neither release from sin and its guilt nor the remission of the due and merited punishment for sins.*

> ### 1John 2:2
> *Amplified*
> *And He, that same Jesus Himself, is the propitiation (the atoning sacrifice) for our sins, and not for ours alone but also for [the sins of] the whole world.*

Lord I repent for every sin & I apply the blood of Jesus & declare:

The Blood of Jesus is Redeeming Me
The Blood of Jesus is Resurrecting Me
The Blood of Jesus has Paid My Debts/Atoned Me
The Blood of Jesus Yield's Life to Me Abundantly

The Blood of Jesus is Purging Me
The Blood of Jesus is Purifying Me
The Blood of Jesus Sanitizes Me
The Blood of Jesus is Sterilizing Me Deeply

The Blood of Jesus has Forgiven Me
The Blood of Jesus Restores My Peace

The Blood of Jesus Sanctifies, Makes Me Whole
The Blood of Jesus Boasts of God's Love for Me

The Blood of Jesus Heals
The Blood of Jesus Strengthens the Essence of My
Individuality
The Blood of Jesus Refreshes, Refines
The Blood of Jesus Fine Tunes & Recaptures My
Destiny

The Blood of Jesus Exposes Bondage that Limits Me
The Blood of Jesus Convicts My Heart
Compassionately
The Blood of Jesus Builds Me Up, & Brings Balance
The Blood of Jesus Acquits Me

The Blood of Jesus Shields
The Blood of Jesus Protects
The Blood of Jesus Nurtures My Soul Wounds
The Blood of Jesus Covers Me in Grace & Mercy

The Blood of Jesus Torments Demons
The Blood of Jesus Breaks, Brings Demons to their
Knees
The Blood of Jesus Judges My Enemies
The Blood of Jesus Reigns With Great Authority

The Blood of Jesus Fills Me
The Blood of Jesus Flows Like Living Water Through
Me
The Blood of Jesus is Power
The Blood of Jesus Produces Miracles Immeasurably

The Blood of Jesus Cinches
The Blood of Jesus Scorches
The Blood of Jesus is a Fiery-Fire Removing Impurities

& the Unnecessary
The Blood of Jesus Smolders the Death & Stench of the
Adversary

The Blood of Jesus Defeats
The Blood of Jesus Defends
The Blood of Jesus Maketh Rich
The Blood of Jesus Breaks Curses While Releasing
Blessings

The Blood of Jesus Speaks Deeply
The Blood of Jesus Has a Voice Profound
The Blood of Jesus is Without Void
The Blood of Jesus Decrees That I Am Free & the
Enemy Is Bound

The Blood of Jesus Endures
The Blood of Jesus Triumphs
The Blood of Jesus Overcomes All
The Blood of Jesus Prevails

The Blood of Jesus
The Blood of Jesus
The Blood of Jesus
Reclaims the Gates of Hell

I AM DRENCHED!
SLOPPY SLOPPY WET!
IN THE MATCHLESS BLOOD OF JESUS!!!

KINGDOM WELLNESS

This decree is inspired by times where I have endured ailments in my body & from insight on healing & warfare obtained through Glory Reign Ministries & Expected End Ministries:

Jeremiah 17:4
KJV
Heal me, O LORD, and I shall be healed; save me, and I shall be saved: for thou art my praise.

The Message
God, pick up the pieces. Put me back together again. You are my praise!

I thank You Lord that You were wounded my transgressions, bruised for my iniquity, that the chastisement of my peace was upon You and by Your stripes I am Healed (Isa 53:5-6).

I thank You Father that what is impossible for man, for doctors, is possible for You Lord (Lu 1:37).

I thank You Jesus that You desire me to prosper and be in good health, even as my soul prosper (3Jn 1:2).

I thank You Lord that greater are You that is in me, residing in my body, than he that is in the world (1Jo 4:4).

And that every word and evil deed, that rises against me, my body, my gifts are condemned by Your presence in me Lord (Isa 54:17).

I bless You for Your blood flowing through my body,

yielding eternal life to every system and organ.

During times of affliction and adversity, I seek You fervently Jesus and decree that many are the afflictions of the righteous but You my healer, delivers me from them all (Psa 34:19).

For when my soul and body is cast down, I will hope in my help which is You Lord. I will praise You, the lifter of my countenance (Psa 45:5).

I decree through the resurrection power of Jesus Christ, I am redeemed from every curse of the law (Gal 3:3). I repent and ask for Your forgiveness Lord of every curse, sin, affliction, sting of death and legal right of the enemy *(Spend time in repentance. Repentance is about turning, a changing of the guard of darkness to God's likeness. Sometimes condemnation keeps us bound to the very thing God is striving to release us from. Therefore, do not focus on what you have done wrong so much as really giving that area over to the Lord).*

I apply Your perfect blood Jesus to my mind, thought life, heart and soul to cleanse me of every sin and wounded issue *(Spend time in this area; deal with any areas the Holy Spirit may show you).*

I decree that my atmosphere and home are being cleansed even now by Your blood and I invite the Holy Spirit and all His attributes to come and abide eternally in my natural home and atmosphere even as He already lives and dwells in me (1Cor 6:19).

I repent Jesus of any generational or personal areas of offense, unforgiveness, anger, rejection, covetousness, pride, bitterness, fear, stress, worry, hatred, double-mindedness *(Repent as the Holy Spirit reveals to sources of affliction to you).*

In your mighty name Jesus, I break every self-inflicted curse, word curses spoken by others, family curse, witchcraft curse, witchcraft prayers, curses spoken via manipulation and control, curses of religious and traditional bondage, and any other curses knowingly or unknowingly in operation in my life.

In Your name Jesus, I fall out of agreement with these curses and fall out of agreement with every ungodly covenant, agreement, and soultie. I repent for any legal rights they have to me, and decree that the covenants and soulties are null and void, broken and detached from me with no way of ever mending; and loose the blood of Jesus as a sealed wall between them and me in Jesus name.

Even as you have taught my hands to war and my fingers to fight, I declare restoration to the wearing and tearing of my hands and my body in general (Psa 144:1). I decree replenishment of power to my hands and fingers and fresh authority in my gifts to demolish the camp of the enemy.

Even as you have given me the kingdom everywhere the souls of my feet tread, I speak healing to my feet and restoration of all damage that has been done spiritually and naturally as I treaded and conquered cursed land (Deu11:24). I pull out the thorns of walking on accursed land, and decree blessings in Jesus name to my feet and shod my feet with fresh weaponry of the gospel of peace and power to further snuff out wickedness while conquering over all the power of the enemy.

23

I loose the fire of the Holy Spirit to melt any demonic weapons that may be lodged in any area of my body in the name of Jesus.

I command all venom, poison, affliction, pain, ungodly growths and tumors and every other affects these demonic weapons have caused to dry up at the root, and be cinched to nothing (to death) by the fire of the Holy Spirit now in the name of Jesus.

I spend time soaking my mind, thoughts, will, and soul in the refiner's fire of the Dunamis power of God to bring virtue into my body and to melt away all war wounds and demonic weaponry (*I suggest you do this on a regular basis*).

I speak healing and proper heavenly alignment to each system in my body: I decree wellness to my:

o Muscular System
o Nervous System
o Reproductive System
o Skeletal System
o Endocrine System

o Lymphatic System
o Immune System
o Circulatory System
o Respiratory System
o Urinary System
o Digestion System

I decree that every organ in my body is healthy and working properly. I apply the miracle power of God to any organ that needs healing, recreation, and/or resurrection in the name of Jesus. Eternal life comes to every organ in my body in the name of Jesus.

I speak the might, strength and power of God to my muscles, tendons, ligaments, tissue, and command them in the name of Jesus to be healthy, supernaturally vital, self-rejuvenating and whole.

I decree my natural body is clothed daily in the might of Christ. I put on Christ and I walk inside His image, living inside my eternal body and life that He has restored unto me.

Lord You blessed me and said I am to be fruitful, and multiply, and replenish the earth, and subdue it: and have dominion over the fish of the sea, over the fowl of the air, and over every living thing that moves upon the earth (Gen 1:28). I take dominion through King Jesus over my spiritual and natural reproduction system and decree barrenness, abortion, premature death, tragedy, has no place in my existence.

I decree I produce spiritually and naturally with ease and establish the kingdom in my spiritual and natural womb commanding it to flourish and produce eternal fruit that my lineage can continually gleam from.

I subdue healthiness in body and in the land and decree replenishment where necessary to establish Your kingdom in my midst.

I decree impotence is not my lot and I am able to produce spiritually and naturally for the building up of God's kingdom.
I decree that the fouls of the air, the prince in the air, weather spirits, and all unhealthiness in my atmosphere is subject to Your dominion over and in me and will not bind and afflict my body in anyway. I release You King Jesus, to push out the rulership of darkness in these areas of my life and to reign in my body in the name of Jesus.

I decree that I abide under the secret place of You Lord,

and declare Psalms 91 is my banner against demons
that attempt to attack my body because of my ministry.

I decree that when I speak healing comes immediately
to me and those I minister with and to.

I bless You for my body's ability to heal itself. I decree
this gift of being able to heal myself is consistently
active in my body on a daily basis, and is keeping me
well.

I thank You Jesus that You have taken away every
sickness of Egypt (Deu 7:15).

I decree every place that the enemy has sought to steal
in my life or body, You Jesus, have restored it. I decree
I will live a long, prosperous, and abundant life
physically and spiritually (Jn 10:10).

I decree that Psa 91 is encompassing me, no tragedy
comes to my body. It sustains the gifts that are within
me. No evil is befalling them and angels are guarding
me.

I decree that the glory light of God is breaking forth at
Your appointed time and my health is speedily
springing forth as Your righteousness is before me and
Your glory is my reward (Isa 58:8).

Even as the woman with the issue of blood touched the
helm of Your garment and was made whole, I reach
out and touch You today and decree wholeness is
overwhelming my being in the name of Jesus.

I decree that all my gifts are healed because my body,
mind, and soul are healed. I am a complete

representation of journeying in the fullness of Salvation and being an heir to Your throne.

I GOT THE KEYS, LOOSE MY THANGS!

Matthew 16:19
Amplified
I will give you the keys of the kingdom of heaven; and whatever you bind (declare to be improper and unlawful) on earth must be what is already bound in heaven; and whatever you loose (declare lawful) on earth must be what is already loosed in heaven.

KJV
And I will give unto thee the keys of the kingdom of heaven: and whatsoever thou shalt bind on earth shall be bound in heaven: and whatsoever thou shalt loose on earth shall be loosed in heaven.

Lord, You have given me the keys to the kingdom of heaven and with these keys, the power to bind and to loose.

I bless You for my keys and decree the enemy is unlawful in my sphere of influence at all times and that Your dominion King Jesus, is the law in my sphere of influence at all times, especially as I surrender to You in my ministry.

I decree that my ministry binds sickness and unlocks health.

I decree that I bind up incurable diseases and unlock cures and miracles as I exalt You Jesus.

I decree that I bind up demonic plans of the enemy and

unlock strategies to bring his plans to shame and death as You roar through me Lord.

I decree that poverty, poverty cycles, lack, and just enough are bound in the name of Jesus; I release the wealth of Your kingdom Jesus via my gifts to those I minister to and minister with.

I decree that prosperity in mind, body, emotions, will, soul, and finances are released to me, my family and friends, and those I am ministering with and to.

I decree slavery, fear, mockery, fear of man, shame, and every other restricting demon is bound up and freedom and liberation of praise and worship is released unto You Lord via my life and ministry.

I decree that as I walk in my gifting, chains are loosed and prison doors are open just as it was when Paul and Silas were in prison.
I decree religion, tradition, and man's programs are bound and slung out of the territory till judgment day as I glorify You Jesus through my ministry.

I decree mental illness, double-mindedness....Legion...is bound and snuffed out of Your people eternally as I declare Your Lordship through my ministry.

I decree strongholds and demonic kingdoms are bound together, loosed to the feet of Jesus with fear and trembling, and the covenant between You and Your people are restored as I war through my ministry gifts.

I decree hardness of heart, stubborn wills, and sin strongholds are bound and Godly conviction and repenting mindsets breakout everywhere as I minister for You Jesus.

I decree rivers flow from heaven and people are filled with Your precious Holy Spirit and desire spiritual and water baptism as You flow through my gifts.

Jesus, I decree the enemy is bound, declared unlawful and Glory for You is released and loosed in all the earth as I yield You abandoned Glory through my life and ministry.

SET APART FOR KINGDOM ADVANCEMENT

Let's specifically address perversion because it is the one area aside from religion and tradition that keeps the ministry from going forth in a pure vein where people can truly be transformed and where God can be effectively glorified. Perversion can be an impure motive or a crooked act and can range from ungodly heart issues to sexual immorality.

Flesh and sin simply cannot glory in the presence of the Lord (1Cor 1:29) so when the presence of the Lord manifests, it exposes darkness...even darkness within us as ministers. If there is any sin issue in our lives, especially those that we fail to acknowledge or work on releasing to God, it will manifest in our ministry. How we take care of our Spirit and what we expose ourselves to, determines how effectively God can utilize us in ministry for His glory. We want God to be edified as we go forth in His name, so let's just decree that we shall be set apart for kingdom advancement.

Colossians 3:5
Amplified
kill (deaden, deprive of power) the evil desire lurking in your members [those animal impulses and all that is earthly in you that is employed in sin]: sexual vice, impurity, sensual appetites, unholy desires, and all greed and covetousness, for that is idolatry (the deifying of self and other created things instead of God).

KJV
Mortify therefore your members which are upon the earth; fornication, uncleanness, inordinate affection, evil concupiscence, and covetousness, which is idolatry:

KJV
But know that the LORD hath set apart him that is godly for himself: the LORD will hear when I call unto him. Stand in awe, and sin not: commune with your own heart upon your bed, and be still. Selah. Offer the sacrifices of righteousness, and put your trust in the LORD.

In the name of Jesus, I decree I am not of this world, and therefore I do not conform to the matters of this world, hell, or the grave has to offer (Rom 12:2).

I unyieldingly renounce the lust of the flesh, the lust of the eyes and the pride of life and decree they have no place in my ministry or life in general (1Jo 2:16-19).

I deaden and deprive of power, any ungodly desire lurking in any area of my mind, body, soul, personality, character, will, atmosphere, and decree I shall not fulfill the lust of the flesh and decree my flesh is subject to my spirit (Gal 5:16).

I rebuke and command a loosing of myself from all sensual appetites, unholy desires, unhealthy longing or wooing of the enemy, and any forms of inordinate affections which are rooted in idolatry for I do not serve idols; I serve Jesus Christ the only true and living Lord and Savior (Col 3:5).

I decree I am led of the Holy Spirit and if it is not in

heaven, it CANNOT be in my life (Eph 2:6).

According to Gal 5:19-21 and 1Cor 6:7-11, adultery, fornication, homosexuality, sodomy, idolatry, effeminacy, uncleanness, lasciviousness, hatred, variance, emulations, wrath, strife, seditions, heresies, envyings, thievery, covetous, murders, drunkenness, revellings (taking pleasure in drinking or partying) and the like are not a part of the kingdom of heaven; I therefore, renounce them from my ministry, my life, and lineage.

In the name of Jesus, I repent for any indulgence in these acts personally and generationally, I decree I have been washed and sanctified by the blood of Jesus and claim my justification and inheritance into God's kingdom through Jesus Christ (1Cor 6:11-20)

I decree I will no longer sin against my own body and even as I uncompromisingly flee from these acts, I loose the vengeance of Jesus to eternally run them away from my life (1Cor 6:18).

I decree a lifestyle of striving to hate the things that God hates. I therefore command my flesh, soul, mind, heart, personality, and character to fall out of agreement with proud looks, lying, spiritual, physical and emotional acts that shed innocent blood, a heart that plots evil, feet that runs to mischief, false witnessing that breathes lies, and the sowing of strife and discord (Pro 6:16-19).

I decree that to the pure all things are pure and I ask the Holy Spirit for an immediate conviction and a repentant heart anytime impure motives manifest in me or others (Tit 1:15).

I decree I am not desirous of vain glory, provoking of others, and cast down jealousy and covetous (Gal 5:26).

I renounce the spirits and heritage of lust and perversion and decree my ministry and giftings in general will never be used for evil enticements and endeavors and for personal gain.

I decree God is my judge. He is the one who putteth down one and setteth up another (Psa 75:7).

In the name of Jesus, I fall out of agreement with the spirit of entertainment and close every door and effort to use my ministry and giftings in general as performance or to fill program space.

I decree the enemy CANNOT have my gifts and calling. I wash my gifts from all contamination of the world and the demonic kingdom and rededicate every gift back to God (spending time cleansing and rededicating each gift to God).

Though I have been called to save souls, I will not succumb to ungodly acts or use the mandate to save others as a justification to participate in sin.

I decree I consecrate myself before God and daily strive to be holy as God is holy (Lev 11:44, 1Pe 1:16).

I decree that I forgive anyone that has abused or taken advantage of me sexually. I turn them over to the Lord, my ultimate avenger, and I eternally close every portal and gateway that was open in my life to the spirit of perversion (Mat 5:44:45).

I renounce, cast out, and eternally fall out of agreement with the offender spirit and forgive myself and ask for forgiveness Lord of any times I have taken advantage of others sexually or otherwise. Bless them Father, submerge them in Your blood and purify and heal them of any sin and wounds my actions created (Mat 6:9).

I reclaim my purity through the sanctity of Jesus and take back every illegal right of the enemy to violate me further by having me engage in behaviors and activities that came through the defilement of evil (Mat 6:8).

I decree I walk uprightly and fear the Lord with a Holy reverence. I therefore, cast off perverse ways and despise them even as God despises them (Pro 14:2).

I enmesh with the fruit of the Holy Spirit which is love, joy, peace, longsuffering, gentleness, goodness, faith, meekness, and temperance, and decree they have become a tangible part of me (Gal 5:22-23).

I crucify my flesh consistently with prayer, the word, fasting, and declare that I minister and journey in the pure spirit and image of Christ (Gal 5:27).

I decree I exude a focused will and mindset that is in pursuit of my ordained destiny, and I am set apart for the will and purpose of advancing and establishing God's kingdom in the earth realm.

ACCOUNTABILITY DECREES

1Peter 1:14-17
Amplified
[Live] as children of obedience [to God]; do not conform yourselves to the evil desires [that governed you] in your former ignorance [when you did not know the requirements of the Gospel]. But as the One Who called you is holy, you yourselves also be holy in all your conduct and manner of living. For it is written, You shall be holy, for I am holy.

Message
Don't lazily slip back into those old grooves of evil, doing just what you feel like doing. You didn't know any better then; you do now. As obedient children, let yourselves be pulled into a way of life shaped by God's life, a life energetic and blazing with holiness. God said, "I am holy; you be holy." You call out to God for help and he helps — he's a good Father that way. But don't forget, he's also a responsible Father, and will not let you get by with sloppy living.

John 12:26
Amplified
If anyone serves Me, he must continue to follow Me [to cleave steadfastly to Me, conform wholly to My example in living and, if need be, in dying] and wherever I am, there will My servant be also. If anyone serves Me, the Father will honor him.

Message
If any of you wants to serve me, then follow me. Then you'll be where I am, ready to serve at a moment's

notice. The Father will honor and reward anyone who serves me.

I repent for any disobedience and ask for Your forgiveness, Lord and another chance to do your will.

I come into agreement with obedience and align myself with the plans You have for my destiny and the destiny of my lineage.

I deny myself for the sake of God and His kingdom. Me, Myself, and I are cast down and the Father, Son and the Holy Ghost are exalted in its place.

I use my gifts when God says so and am disciplined in imparting into my gifts by praying, fasting, reading my word, etc. (*Continue to name those things that are conducive to the betterment of your gifts*).

I do NOT walk in my gifts when I feel like it, am touched by God's presence, or when I am happy. I minister through the scripture Psa 150:6 that states let everything that has breath praise the Lord. So I give God due praise despite how I feel, despite the sacrifices and at the expense of myself and flesh.

I do not allow my flesh or emotions to run my life or ministry. My flesh is dead and my emotions are balanced. My flesh and emotions are submitted and committed to being in order with the presence of the Lord and are a blessing and not a curse to my gifts or ministry.

I do not fear man and do not become scared or intimidated when I go forth in ministry. I ascend into the kingdom of heaven and minister before Your throne Lord. Your open heaven is my secret place and I minister in a glow of favored abandonment under Your feathers Lord.

I do not limit myself as I flow limitlessly in and with God. Every part of my body is healed with wholeness, functions properly, and is in line with God's image. Because my body is a temple of the Holy Ghost and member in Christ Jesus, My body is healthy and fit and functioning at the ultimate capacity to producing God's will and glory.

My gifts are submitted to God, to leadership, the vision of my church, and the ministry and vision of my personal calling and the ministry team to which I belong.

I minister in sync and in unified agreement with those I minister with. I accept them, see them as God sees them and esteem them as He desires them to be.

I am in unity with my ministry team in the spirit and natural realm and invest all my gifts as God leads, into my ministry and the body of Christ in general for the building and establishment of God's kingdom.

I pray for my ministry team and church, and they pray for me. I believe in who they are in God, and they believe in me. Who we are complements who God is and desires us to be. I renounce backsliding and understand that my actions don't just affect me but my team, my church, the body of Christ, and the vision of our ministry.

Everything about my ministry, from the investment of my time, finances, prayer, fasting, and obedience, is done through a spirit of excellence, yields glory to God, and works together for my good and the good of those I minister to and with.

I am supernatural and I do not take my ministry lightly. I am responsible and accountable to my ministry and everything God has granted to my hands.

I study to show myself approved and I press with a great yearning...a great passion...to the prize of the High calling of Jesus! I am in Jesus and He is in me. Jesus is my reasonable service. My gifts (*Begin naming your gifts*) are my service to Jesus.

FIVEFOLD MINISTRY

Jesus gave the fivefold ministry to the body of Christ for the purposes of building up the body, and effectively equipping the saints to minister salvation, healing, deliverance and wholeness, which signs following. It is essential that we transition from works and operating in giftings, to operating in our ordained calling, so that we can effectively save souls, strategically impact people's lives, shift and enhance communities and nations, such that the fullness of the kingdom of heaven can be established in the earth realm.

Ephesians 4:11-12
Amplified
And His gifts were varied; He Himself appointed and gave men to us] some to be apostles (special messengers), some prophets (inspired preachers and expounders), some evangelists (preachers of the Gospel, traveling missionaries), some pastors (shepherds of His flock) and teachers. His intention was the perfecting and the full equipping of the saints (His consecrated people), that they should do] the work of ministering toward building up Christ's body (the church),

Verse 7-13
Message
But that doesn't mean you should all look and speak and act the same. Out of the generosity of Christ, each of us is given his own gift. The text for this is, He climbed the high mountain, He captured the enemy and seized the booty, He handed it all out in gifts to the people. Is it not true that the One who

climbed up also climbed down, down to the valley of earth? And the One who climbed down is the One who climbed back up, up to highest heaven. He handed out gifts above and below, filled heaven with his gifts, filled earth with his gifts. He handed out gifts of apostle, prophet, evangelist, and pastor-teacher to train Christ's followers in skilled servant work, working within Christ's body, the church, until we're all moving rhythmically and easily with each other, efficient and graceful in response to God's Son, fully mature adults, fully developed within and without, fully alive like Christ.

I decree God has given me to mankind and that He gave me as a gift, yet I operate in my ordained calling.

I decree in Jesus name that I shift this day from giftings to calling, from operating in works to moving in Godly destiny, from operating under fear of man to surrendering to the fear of God.

I decree I am who God says I am and I declare to the heavenlies and earth realm that God has designed and called me to be (*State what God has said about you*) and has sent me for the perfecting and equipping of the saints and the building up and establishment of His kingdom.

In Jesus name I bind religion and tradition and command their shackles to loose me and my calling in the name of Jesus.

In the name of Jesus, I bind religious and traditional mindsets, manipulations, and controls and I fall out of agreement with them and their effects on any part of my existence in the name of Jesus.

I decree a renewing of my mind regarding the body of Christ, being God's bride and His heavenly kingdom in the name of Jesus.

I decree I am being transformed by the renewing of my mind and my thought processes are under the subjection of Jesus. You, Lord God, are the chief Apostle, and I align with You and those who are following You.

For according to Mat 13:11, it has been given unto me by Jesus to know the mysteries of the kingdom of heaven, but to them (those that are not of Him), it is not given.

Lu 8:10 further asserts that Jesus has given me a desire to know the mysteries of the kingdom of God: but to others in parables; that seeing they might not see, and hearing they might not understand. I decree that as a kingdom builder and establisher, I see and I hear...Jesus reveals unto to me the mysteries of His kingdom.

In your name Jesus, I decree my gift of (*name you gifts individually*) establishes the kingdom of heaven, shift atmospheres, prophecies, witnesses, teaches, and shepherds Your flock.

I decree that just like the apostles and disciples in the Bible, signs follow me when I minister.

I decree Isa 11:2 with contention that the spirit of the LORD rests upon me, the spirit of wisdom and understanding, the spirit of counsel and might, the spirit of knowledge and of the fear of the LORD.

42

I decree that as I minister wisdom, understanding, counsel, might, knowledge and fear of the Lord, captivates the people and resonates in the atmosphere.

I decree that I have no reason to be jealous or covetous for my unique giftings and callings are needed in the kingdom of God. I work rhythmically with my brothers and sisters to mature the body to look, think and act like Christ.

I speak apostolic and prophetic growth to all God requires of me and particularly to my ministry. I cast off immaturity and arise inside the apostolic mandate bringing transformation in all God leads my hands to do.

I therefore consecrate and set apart myself for God, and share in the heavenly calling, and I declare Heb 3:1 while thoughtfully and attentively considering Jesus, the Apostle and High Priest whom I confessed as my King, embracing my call into this Christian faith.

MIRACLES, SIGNS & WONDERS

I declare the scripture Psalms 2:7 - The Lord has given me the nations for my inheritance, and the ends of the earth for my possession.

Just like Stephen in Acts 6:8 The Lord has filled me with faith and power and supernatural ability to do great wonders and miracles among the people.

I bless You Lord for Your power in Paul in Acts 19:11-12. And I decree that I too have been empowered with special miracles, such that from my body is brought unto the sick handkerchiefs and aprons, and as I transfer your power in them and they are distributed to the people, diseases depart from them, and evil spirits leave out of them.

For the Message Version of the Bible asserts that you Lord did powerful things through Paul, things quite out of the ordinary. I decree that You Lord do powerful things quite out of the ordinary through me. Just like with Paul, the word will get around and people will start taking pieces of clothing - handkerchiefs and scarves and the like - that had touched my skin and then touching the sick with them, the touch will do it – that they are and will be healed and whole.

I decree that these extraordinary miracles happen because I believe. As Jn 14:12 asserts that because I believe in Jesus, the works that He did, I shall do also and even greater works because He has gone unto the Father.

And Just like You Jesus did the disciples in Mat 10:7-8, You have sent me to the world to preach, saying, the kingdom of heaven is at hand. I heal the sick, cleanse the lepers, raise the dead, cast out devils: freely I have received, freely I give.

I therefore walk in the authority of Lu 9:2 and declare that You Jesus have given me power and authority over all devils, and to cure diseases. And You send me to preach the kingdom of God, and to heal the sick.

I decree through the authority of Lu 10:9 that You allow me to heal the sick that are therein, and say unto them, "The kingdom of God is come nigh unto you!"

For I have received power of Acts 1:8. I declare that the fullness of the Holy Ghost has come upon me: and I am a witness of Your resurrection power with miracles, signs, and wonders following me unto Jerusalem, and in all Judaea, and in Samaria, and unto the uttermost part of the earth.

For through Your Dunamis power, I decree a thing, and it is established unto me: and the light of God shines upon my ways (Job 22:28).
For the Message Version of Job 22:27-28 declares, I take delight in God, the Mighty One, and look to Him joyfully and boldly. I pray to Him and He listens; He helps me do what I've promised. I decide what I want and it will happen; for my life is bathed in light.

I decree in Jesus name that my life is bathed in His life. I can do all things through Christ who strengthens me (Phi 4:13).

For I decree I am Your kingdom shifter, I carry and establish your kingdom and glory Lord.

I am as Moses was in Deu 11:24; every place that the sole of my foot shall tread upon, God has given it to me.

I stand in Mal 4:3 and declare that in Your name Jesus, tread down the wicked; and they shall be ashes under the soles of my feet.

I am more than a conqueror according to Ro 8:37. I am a victorious eternal conqueror.

As Lu 10:19 contends, "God have given me power to tread on serpents and scorpions, and over all the power of the enemy: and nothing shall by any means hurt me."

So I marinate in Ps 91:13 and decree that I tread upon the lion and adder: the young lion and the dragon I trample under my feet.

And I thus declare Eph 3:20, "The Lord is able to do exceeding abundantly above all that I ask or think, according to the power that worketh in me....limitless Dunamis and Ezousia power worketh in me."

DISMANTLING STRONGHOLDS

In the name of Jesus, my ministry transforms atmospheres, climates, cities, nations, and generations.

In Your name Lord, I enter the spirit realm to do damage in the devil's kingdom. God You said everywhere the soles of my feet tread is given unto me. Every time I minister, I take up ground and territory for the kingdom (Deu 11:24).

As I tread upon the wicked and they are ashes under the soles of my feet, I decree my ministry dismantles the enemy and gives me and God's people his lot and everything he has stolen legally and illegally (Mal 4:3).

My ministry treads upon the lion and addler, the young lion and dragon are trampled to destruction under my feet (Psa 91:13).

My feet are submitted to the rhythm, warfare, intercession, instructive, and destructive movement of Jesus. My ministry increases with power, and tread upon scorpions and serpents and over all the power of the enemy; I do harm and damage to the enemy; nothing harms me (Lu 10:19).

When I minister, in the name of Jesus, I run through troops and leap over walls. I dismantle the enemy and triumph in destiny (2Sam 22:30).

Every spirit in the 2nd heaven, hell, grave, earth, atmosphere, and in people, are subject to my ministry (Lu 10:20).

Any evil that binds me and your people flee and never return as I go forth in ministry (Jam 4:7).

As You teach my hands to war Lord, grace and precision manifest through me and shows forth the power, authority, and transformation of Your glory (Psa 144:1).

Because of the name and power of Jesus in me, miracles, signs, wonders, and greater works manifest through me as I minister (Phi 2:9-11).

People are saved, delivered, healed and set free to wholeness as I declare Your great name Jesus…the name that is above every name…the name that every knee must bow and tongue must confess that Jesus is Lord unto the glory of God My Father. Jesus is Lord and King over my life and ministry! (Phi 2:9-11).

GODLY VENGEANCE ROAR

Psalms 146
Amplified
Let the high praises of God be in their throats and a two-edged sword in their hands, to wreak vengeance upon the nations and chastisement upon the peoples, to bind their kings with chains, and their nobles with fetters of iron, to execute upon them the judgment written. He [the Lord] is the honor of all His saints. Praise the Lord! (Hallelujah!)

Psalms 94:1-2
Amplified
O LORD God, You to Whom vengeance belongs, O God, You to Whom vengeance belongs, shine forth! Rise up, O Judge of the earth; render to the proud a fit compensation!

Deuteronomy 32:43
Amplified
Rejoice, O ye nations, [with] his people: for he will avenge the blood of his servants, and will render vengeance to his adversaries, and will be merciful unto his land, [and] to his people.

Ezekial 25:17
Amplified
And I will execute great vengeance upon them with furious rebukes; and they shall know that I [am] the LORD, when I shall lay my vengeance upon them.

Nahum 1:2-3 *(study this chapter as it will transform your mind about the vengeance of God)*

Amplified
The Lord is a jealous God and avenging; the Lord avenges and He is full of wrath. The Lord takes vengeance on His adversaries and reserves wrath for His enemies. The Lord is slow to anger and great in power and will by no means clear the guilty.

Message
God is serious business. He will not be trifled with. He avenges his foes. He stands up against his enemies, fierce and raging. But God doesn't lose his temper. He's powerful, but it's a patient power.

I decree that as I go forth in Jesus, the high praises of God are in my mouth, and a two-edged sword operates in my hands.

I decree that as I minister, God who is in me, wreaks vengeance upon the demonic nations and chastisement upon the enemy, yielding complete ability to declare His entrance.

I decree the Lord's vengeance has consumed my very stance and is binding demonic kings with chains, and their nobles with fetters of iron.

I decree the Lord's vengeance saturates me and is executing judgment against the powers of darkness, while declaring His honor, His Lordship, among all saints and all mankind.

I decree that as Jesus drenches & encompass my gift of (*name your gifts*), He is inflicting and humiliating the enemy, and is unleashing Godly violent revenge upon his camp.

I decree recompense is coming to the proud as I move forth through His vengeance as none get away...I Trample! I Trample! My feet become kingdom establishers...heavenly lamps!

Counterblow after counterblow is released in retribution against the enemy as God wages war as I minister.

Even as I rejoice & shout for joy, my God, the avenger, administers vengeance upon the wicked, dismantling his treacherous plans.

I decree my high praise loose the vengeance of the Lord to tear down high places and crumble demonic altars to nothing.

God shakes demons with a fierce vengeance as I exalt Him with a clean heart.

His wrath downpours and the earthquakes in trembling awe as the Lord roars ferociously...Demons turn in on themselves when taking flight as my chastiser boasts His righteous indignation as only He can.

I decree that as I minister people will know that You are in charge of them and You truly care. They will see Your vengeance in my (*name your gifts*): Your jealousy, Your Love, as Your dominion is recklessly dispatched and undoubtedly declared.

GODLY VENGEANCE ROAR THROUGH MY MINISTRY!!!!

HEAVEN'S ANOINTING OIL

Anoint my mind, vision, and imagination Lord, so that I can receive downloads from You easily in every area of my existence and be able to translate what I see through my ministry.

Anoint my ability to esteem and encourage others Lord so I may be able to impart gifts with ease that roots and breeds supernatural acceleration such that what would have taken years to cultivate only takes minutes to capture.

Anoint my memory Lord so I can remember what You show me, remember what I hear in prayer and hear via the Holy Spirit, that I may learn Your message and flow with effortless power and authority.

Lord, teach me how to become the gift(s) that I am operating in and let me learn with zeal and passion until what has been released out of You Lord, becomes a synchronized part of me.

Anoint my spirit Lord so I will grow in some fashion every time I utilize my gifts and as I praise and worship You, my mighty Lord and King.

Anoint this vessel Lord so that I will flow with precision and grace in the spirit and speak the oracles of Your message.

Anoint my feet Lord so they might take up territory for your kingdom everywhere that I tread, and will be free to follow Your path with liberty.

Anoint my character Lord so it commands atmospheres, climates, people, and demons. Allow me to tread in royal stature while anointing my personality with humility to be able to walk worthy but respectfully and humbly, within the favor that radiates from my life.

Anoint my will and personality Lord so that I can bring forth Your message with confidence and boldness; not fearing the eyes and likes of man, but only caring that I please and am the best example of who You are, while exuding Your godly fruit.

Position me inside Your anointing Lord, stretch Your arm over me. Be my bubble that I thrive within, so that I can minister only through Your glory and fullness Lord.

HOLY BOLDNESS

I can do all things in each area of my giftings through Christ who strengthens me (Phi 4:19).

There is not anything that I cannot do and no task that I cannot complete with ease because greater is He that is in me than He that is in the world (1Jo 4:4).

I am the elect of God and established to the end. Therefore, I am worthy to worship before Him and worthy to minister for Him (Col 3:12).

I am dead to sin and made nigh by the blood of Jesus. The blood of Jesus runs through my veins and is purifying me daily to minister before and for my King (Ro 6:11).

I am crucified with Christ and joint heir with Him. Christ is synchronized in one accord with and through me. I reign in my life and ministry as I walk in my rightful place with Him (Gal 2:20).

My body is a temple of Jesus Christ. The Holy Spirit dwells in and upon me. I do not have to conjure up God's presence as it already dwells inside of me and moves through me (1Cor 6:15).

I triumph in Christ. I triumph in my giftings. Victory is mine when I minister. I overcome all evil with good when I walk in my gifts (2Cor 2:14).

I am a partaker of Christ. I put on Christ. Christ in me is the hope of glory. My ministry brings people hope while giving God glory (Heb 3:14).

No weapon formed against me shall prosper. For my weapons of warfare are not carnal but mighty through God to the pulling down of strongholds. Through my gifts, I dismantle demonic strongholds (Isa 54:14).

As I minister, I tread upon serpents and scorpions and over all the power of the enemy. Nothing the enemy does can harm me as I am trampling the wiles of the devil through my ministry (Lu10:19).

I do not have a spirit of fear but love power and a sound mind. I am sound in my giftings. I am sound in my concept of ministry concerning my gifts. The power of God in me, makes me complete in my ministry (2Tim 1:7).

I am free to be me. I minister inside the freedom, the liberation of the Holy Spirit and His anointing encompasses me (1Co 2:17).

KINGDOM RELATIONSHIPS
Healthiness in Marriage, Family, & Friendships

1Corinthians 13:4-7
Amplified
Love endures long and is patient and kind; love never is envious nor boils over with jealousy, is not boastful or vainglorious, does not display itself haughtily. It is not conceited (arrogant and inflated with pride); it is not rude (unmannerly) and does not act unbecomingly. Love (God's love in us) does not insist on its own rights or its own way, for it is not self-seeking; it is not touchy or fretful or resentful; it takes no account of the evil done to it [it pays no attention to a suffered wrong]. It does not rejoice at injustice and unrighteousness, but rejoices when right and truth prevail. Love bears up under anything and everything that comes, is ever ready to believe the best of every person, its hopes are fadeless under all circumstances, and it endures everything [without weakening]. Love never fails [never fades out or becomes obsolete or comes to an end].

I decree the fullness of God's covenant is operating in my marriage, family and friendships, and that my love continually grows, and never fades, becomes obsolete or comes to an end.

I decree that only the relationships God has ordained for me will be in my life and that they are enduring, burden bearing, and have the best interest of all parties involved.

I renounce division and discord and decree it has no

56

place in my household and relationships (Pro 18:24).

I renounce deception, need to control, passive aggressiveness, double-mindedness, and manipulation and decree truthful, godly communication that breeds godly resolution, godly love and compassion and kingdom results (Eph 4:15).

I bind distractions and draining spirits and personalities, and decree an immediate quickening to discern when they are in operation through me and in my life.

I fall out agreement with unhealthy relationships and imbalanced interactions and promise to let go when God leads, and to make personal and relational improvements when the Holy Spirits requires it of me and my relationships (1Cor 15:33).

I decree I will not be inordinate and familiar in my relationships and interactions by getting sensual needs met through having people play roles in my life that are not of God's design. I decree I will flow through the Spirit of God to get my needs met and be in order with who He says people are in my life and what my interactions with them are to be (Col 3:5).

I decree wholeness within myself first and decree I will constantly pursue the face of God so His image can be effectively established in me (Rom 13:14).

I decree wholeness and healthiness within marriage, family, friendships and interactions with others (Eph 4:9-10).

I decree offense, unforgiveness, anger, bitterness,

57

rejection, pride (*Name others as the Holy Spirit reveals them to you*) has no place in me. I search myself and immediately repent and forgive when necessary (Heb 10:24, Eph 4:32).

I decree I repent quickly and express my faults without giving into pride, shame or guilt, as these only lead to self-condemnation which is not of God (Jam 5:16)

I decree my love is not self-seeking, it's not easily angered, it keeps no record of wrong (1Cor 13:5).

I decree I have the eyes and mind of Christ and do not continually focus on the faults and issues of others, but see others through His eyes and mind, and esteem them accordingly (Eph 1:18, Rom 12:12).

I decree I am able to express my thoughts and feelings in a healthy manner that esteem others higher than myself, and am a constant encouragement to those in my life (1Thes 5:11).

I decree I am able to give and receive constructive criticism and am open to searching myself for the benefits and improvements of my marriage, family, friendships and life in general (Heb 10:25).

I decree in the name of Jesus that I walk in unity in my marriage (Amos 3:3).

I decree in the name of Jesus that I have left the covering of my parents and now cleave to my mate (Gen 2:24).

I decree a healthy prayer life for my household and that we confirm to what Jesus is speaking to us for the advancement of our lineage (Jam 5:16).

I decree that what God has said about my marriage, my mate, me personally, our lineage, and destiny is so and will come to pass in Jesus name.

I renounce the spirit of divorce, abortion, and miscarriage and decree it has no place in my marriage and family line.

I renounce the spirit of Jezebel and decree I will not operate in her attributes or succumb to her presence in others.

I decree a commitment to be balanced regarding ministry and home responsibilities (Rom 12:10).

I decree to take time of devotion and care to my marriage, family, and friendships (1Cor 12:25)

As iron sharpens iron, I decree I sharpen the countenance of my mate, family, and friends (Pro 27:17).

I bind my relationships to the love of Christ and loose His ability to love unconditionally to our hearts and actions (1Cor 13).

KINGDOM WEALTH

I decree my ministry and every other ministry God grants to my hands are successful and that I have more than enough to fund each vision.

I decree that lack and poverty are not my lot. I bind them and loose them from my life and sphere of influence in the name of Jesus!

I decree I am not of this world and am not bound by this world's system. In the name of Jesus, I declare recession, unemployment, foreclosure, high interest rates; downsizing, cutbacks and setbacks of any kind, repossession are not my lot. I decree I am sitting in heavenly places with Christ Jesus and make kingdom decisions regarding my possessions and finances (Eph 2:6).

I decree the spirit of the thief is exposed in my life, family, church, and community; and decree the enemy will not steal my money through afflictions, deceit, tricks of con artists and evil business endeavors (Jn 10:10).

I decree in the name of Jesus that because my house and household are blessed, my neighbors are blessed and our neighborhood resists economic drought and are not subject to famine and economic downturn.

In Jesus name I break every personal and generational curse of lack, just enough, slavery, and poverty, and decree redemption in my finances.

I repent for creating debt and ask for Your forgiveness Father.

I repent for generational debt and all generational sin tied to financial wealth including bad spending habits, stealing, not paying tithes and any other financial sins of my ancestors (Mal 3:10).

I fall out of agreement with frivolous spending, worldly fads, needs to impress man, and slave mentalities, and decree they no longer have control over my will and personality (Rom 12:12).

I apply the blood of Jesus and the healing power of God to any sins and wounded areas on my soul in regards to finances (*Spend time applying the blood & healing power of Jesus to your soul regarding financial sins and wounds*).

I decree that God desires me to prosper and be in good health even as my soul prospers (3Jo 1:2).

I decree wealth and riches are in my house, because I fear You and delight greatly in the commandments of the Lord (Psa 112:1-3)

I decree that I seek first the kingdom of God and His righteousness and all things are added unto me (Matt 6:33).

I decree that because I hearken unto the commandments of the Lord, I am blessed in the city and blessed in the field: blessed in the fruit of my body and the fruit of my ground, the fruit of my beasts (livestock), the increase of my cattle and the young of my flock (Deu 28:4)

I decree, in Jesus name that my baskets and kneading trough are blessed and that I am blessed when I come in and when I go out (Deu 28:5-6).

I decree the Lord has commanded His blessing upon me in my storehouse and in all that I undertake; The Lord has blessed me in the land to which He has ordained for me because I am His and abide under His covenant (Deu 28:8).

I decree that as an heir to the throne, the Lord has called me to a surplus of prosperity. The Lord has done this through the blessing of the fruit of my body, the fruit of my livestock, and ground and in the land which the Lord has promised my lineage (Deu 28:11).

I decree the Lord has opened unto me His good treasury, the heavens and that the heavens rains/reigns, upon my land in due season and pours out abundance blessings into the works of my hands (Deu 28:12).

I bless God for the land and buildings to establish the businesses and ministries He has granted to my hands and the integral and kingdom fruit that will follow these visions.

And even as the Lord has made me the head and not the tail, I decree that because I obey the commandments of the Lord, I am above only, and that being beneath is not my lot (Deu 28:13).

For I decree that Jesus has given me the power and means to get wealth and to maintain it (Deu 8:18).

I decree that the wealth of the wicked is being transferred to me and that the Lord is strategically positioning me to minister to the wealthy (Pro 13:22).

I bless God for wealth, and come into agreement with its flow pouring into my life, and decree that because my debt is under the blood, God is providing countless earth-shattering miracles for me to be debt free and shift to a position of the lender.
For God has created me to be a lender to many nations and not a borrower. I decree I shall be able to sow into others abundantly as God leads for the advancement and establishment of the kingdom (Deu 28:12).

I decree that as I give to others, kingdom overflow is operating in my life in good measure, pressed down, shaken together, running over and returning to me immeasurably as I unselfishly bless others (Lu 6:38).

I agree with God's word that a good man leaves an inheritance that others can glean from. I therefore decree that the spiritual, natural, and financial seeds I sow in life produce eternal kingdom fruit and harvest that blesses my household, church, personal ministry, the poor and the needy and is a part of my lineage from now through eternity (Pro 13:22).

KINGDOM SHIFTERS CHARGE!

Father, we bless You for every person who will be forever changed by the declarations in this book. We decree that they will go forth in power and in victory, declaring Your will in the Earth.

Father, we believe that the declarations contained in this book are atmosphere-shifting, yoke-destroying and life-changing for every believer who dares to speak Your word. We believe that each reader has now been empowered and activated by the Holy Spirit to serve as agents of change, daring to enter the spirit realm and take captive every spiritual blessing, healing, territory and dominion that You have prepared for them.

We decree Your abundant favor upon each of their lives. Bathe them in Your glory, envelope them in Your presence, speak through them, move in them, and cause them to eternally reign with You both now and forevermore.

We furthermore, agree and decree that God has strategically placed territory and lives into your hands to be radically changed for His glory.

Our charge to you is that you will take the tools presented in this book and use them, with the help of the Spirit of God, to advance His kingdom agenda in the earth-realm.

No fear can stop you.

No past can hinder you.

No demon can destroy you.

You are the righteousness of God!

GO FORTH! DECREE THAT THANG & POSSESS THE LAND!

Abundant Blessings, Dr. Angela Smith-Peeples,

Director of Ministry Development

Canaan Christian Church, Louisville, KY

References

Scripture references are from:
www.biblegateway.com
www.blueletterbible.com
www.crosswalk.com

Definitions are quoted from:
www.answers.com
www.m-w.com

Taquetta's Contact Info:

(Website) Kingdomshifters.com
Connect with Taquetta via Facebook & Youtube

Book Picture Cover is by Tashema Davis and Reenita Keys

Kingdom Shifters Books & Apparel

Available at Kingdomshifters.com and Amazon.com

BOOKS FOR EVERYONE

Healing The Wounded Leader	Kingdom Shifters Decree That Thang
There Is An App For That	Kingdom Watchman Builder On the Wall
Embodiment Of A Kingdom Watchman	Dismantling Homosexuality Handbook
Releasing The Vision	Feasting In His Presence

Kingdom Heirs Decree That Thing   Let There Be Sight

Atmosphere Changers (Weaponry)

BOOKS FOR DANCERS

Dancers! Dancers! Decree That Thang

Spirits That Attack Dance Ministers & Ministries

TEE SHIRTS

Kingdom Shifters Tee Shirt	Let The Fruit Speak Tee Shirt
Releasing The Vision Tee Shirt	Kingdom Perspective Tee Shirt
Stand in Position Tee Shirt	No Defense Tee Shirt
My God Rules Like A Boss Tee Shirt	Destiny Blueprint Tee Shirt

CD'S

Decree That Thing CD

Kingdom Heirs Decree That Thing CD

Teachings & Worship CD'